White Cliffs Media Company Performance in World Music Series

Larry W. Smith, Series Editor

- **Drum Damba: Talking Drum Lessons.**
  David Locke.
- **Drum Gahu: The Rhythms of West African Drumming.**
  David Locke.
- **The Music of Santería: Traditional Rhythms of the Batá Drums.**
  John Amira and Steven Cornelius.
- **Salsa!: The Rhythm of Latin Music.**
  Charley Gerard with Marty Sheller.
- **Synagogue Song in America.**
  Joseph A. Levine.
- **Xylophone Music from Ghana.**
  Trevor Wiggins and Joseph Kobom.
- **The Drums of Vodou.**
  Lois Wilcken.

The Music of Santería

Traditional Rhythms of the Batá Drums

John Amira
and
Steven Cornelius

White Cliffs Media Company
Crown Point, IN

White Cliffs Media Company
P.O. Box 561
Crown Point, IN 46307
219-322-5537

Distributed to the book trade by
The Talman Company, Inc.
150 Fifth Avenue
New York, NY 10011
212-620-3182

Library of Congress Catalog Number: 90-12632

Printed on acid-free paper in the United States of America

Library of Congress Cataloging in Publication Data

Amira, John, 1944 -
The music of Santería / John Amira and Steven Cornelius.
p. cm. — (Performance in world music series; no. 5)
Includes bibliographical references and index.
ISBN 0-941677-24-9 (pbk. : alk. paper) : $19.95.
ISBN 0-941677-23-0 (spiral : alk. paper) : $28.95
ISBN 0-9041677-28-1 (cloth : alk. paper) : $39.95.
1. Santería (Cultus) — Music — History and criticism.
2. Blacks — History and criticism. 3. Afro-Americans — Music — History and criticism. 4. Percussion music.
I. Cornelius, Steven, 1952- . II. Title. III. Series.
ML35675.A5 1990
786.9'21796—dc20 90-12632
CP
MN

Contents

Foreword ix

Chapter One

Introduction — 1

Chapter Two

Historical Background — 5

The Religious Context — 5
Synthesis in Cuba — 6
The Foundations of Santería in New York City — 9
Transcription Sources — New York Tradition — 10
Musical and Religious Ideals — 12

Chapter Three

The Instrumental Ensemble — 15

Construction — 15
Tuning — 17
Symbolism — 18

Chapter Four

Musical Structure — 21

The Music Ceremonies — 21
The Oru del Igbodu — 22
The Concept of Clave — 23
The Salutes — 24
Ensemble Performance — 25
Instrumental Roles — 26
Playing Technique — 27

Chapter Five

Transcription and Analysis — 35

Transcription Problems — 35
Eléggua — 37
Ogún — 38
Ochosi — 39
Obaloke — 39

Inle — 40
Babalú Ayé — 40
Osain — 41
Osun — 41
Obatalá — 42
Dadá — 43
Oggué — 43
Agayú — 43
Orula — 43
Oricha Oko — 43
Ibedyi — 44
Changó — 45
Yegguá — 45
Oyá — 45
Ochún — 46
Yemayá — 46
Obba — 47
Odudua — 47

The Oru del Igbodu — Transcriptions — 49

Eléggua — 49
Ogún — 52
Ochosi — 55
Obaloke — 59
Inle — 61
Babalú Ayé — 64
Babalú Ayé (2) — 65
Osain — 67
Osun — 70
Osun (Alternate Version) — 72
Obatalá — 74
Dadá — 79
Oggué — 82
Agayú — 84
Orula — 89
Oricha Oko — 91
Oricha Oko (Alternate Version) — 93
Ibedyi — 96

Changó — 98
Yegguá — 102
Oyá — 104
Ochún — 109
Yemayá — 111
Obba — 118
Odudua — 121

List of Photographs

Photograph 3.1 *Batá drums — traditionally strung set* — 16
Photograph 3.2 *Batá drums — modern tunable set* — 17
Photograph 4.1 *Slap* — 27
Photograph 4.2 *Okónkolo muff* — 28
Photograph 4.3 *Okónkolo tone* — 28
Photograph 4.4 *Itótele muff* — 29
Photograph 4.5 *Iyá muff* — 29
Photograph 4.6 *Itótele tone* — 30
Photograph 4.7 *Iyá tone* — 30
Photograph 4.8 *Enú touch* — 31
Photograph 4.9 *Chachá touch* — 31

List of Figures

Figure 4.1 *The Clave* — 23
Figure 5.1 *Transcription arrangement* — 35
Figure 5.2 *Open enú tone, closed enú tone, enú touch, chachá touch, chachá slap* — 36
Appendix I — Glossary of Lucumí and Spanish Terms — 123
Appendix II — Discography — 125
Annotated Bibliography — 127
Index — 132

Foreword

We have come a long way from the days when aspirant players of the sacred batá in New York City had to piece together their world from copied notes out of Fernando Ortiz' monumental volumes on the instruments of Afro-Cuban music, plus contact with one or two actual Afro-Cuban players of the instruments, plus hard work and constant yearning. The Mariel boatlift from Cuba flooded New York and New Jersey with key masters of the genre. The literature burgeoned. Founding fathers, like Julito Collazo, Carl Vail, Marcus Gordon, and John Amira have seen their world multiply and deepen and become a major current in Afro-Atlantic practice and performance. New York is becoming (after ancient Alexandria, perhaps) the second universal city of the planet and the triumph of the sacred *àwọ́n ilu batá* is part of all that.

In this fine text the reconquest of the voices of the oricha, via the orchestrated cry and thunder of the batá, is told by clear and direct means so that all may comprehend and learn. There is historical background for scholars, notes on construction for practicing musicians, and rich detail on music structure in context for students of performance in African-American studies. Finally, material originating from the texts of Fernando Ortiz, and the memories of Jesús Pérez, Julito Collazo, Puntilla, John Amira, and many, many others are given back to us in richly worked-out transcriptions and analyses of 22 Yoruba-Cuban oricha.

Batá are sacred machines for transubstantiation, moorings for lost vessels of the spirit, sources for percussive symphonies mysteriously generated in the complex interplay of six simultaneously sounding voices, six skins, three pair of hands, one God, many saints, all together, creative, Creator-given. Aché!

Robert Farris Thompson,
Yale University

Chapter One

Introduction

This book presents the salute (or praise) rhythms of batá drumming, the most sacred and complex of the ritual music associated with the Afro-Cuban religion, Santería. Salute rhythms are concise, highly distilled musical prayers, each of which honors and represents a different one of Santería's many gods (*orichas*). Every salute is unique, with its own particular rhythmic and emotional character. Compiled together, the salutes form one of the cornerstones of Afro-Cuban drumming.

This text is written primarily for the performing musician who looks to expand his knowledge of Afro-Cuban music traditions. However, a much wider audience will also find this book rewarding, including: the musicologist who might be interested in the formal structure and mechanics used to generate contemporary batá performance; the practicing Santero who wishes to better understand ritual music; and the general reader seeking an introduction into the music of Santería.

The book is divided into five chapters. Chapter One serves as a general introduction. Chapter Two provides a background into the social history and belief system of Santería. Chapter Three introduces the musical instruments, and Chapter Four discusses general structure and performance techniques. Chapter Five is our primary focus, and consists of musical transcriptions and analyses. The transcriptions, which are designed to serve as models for performance, outline the salutes as they might be heard in religious or folkloric settings.

We have taken a conservative approach in presenting this music by transcribing an older, more traditional performance style than that which is sometimes played by today's most progressive drummers. The transcriptions represent the condensation of mainstream batá drumming styles that have been heard in New York City from the late 1960s to the present.

There is no single correct way to play the batá salutes. Batá drumming is an oral tradition. It lives in the performers' minds rather than on the printed page. Therefore, despite the fact that the rhythms are highly formalized, they are also undergoing constant transformation, and although every authentic performance must conform to basic traditional models, each ensemble will develop its own individual performance style and rhythmic feel.

Today, multiple layers of tradition are being played simultaneously by different ensembles around New York as drummers perform and transmit their knowledge according to their own beliefs concerning authenticity. In short, a study of New York tradition reveals that while there are definitely correct and incorrect ways to play the salute rhythms, to a certain extent each generation, ensemble, and individual performer will internalize and recreate the tradition in his own musical voice.

Due to the above factors it is unlikely that any performance would ever conform exactly with the transcriptions in this book. In some cases where distinct differences in style exist, comparative forms are presented. In others, theoretical models are given because the present styles have certain oddities or inconsistencies that may not have existed in earlier, untraceable forms of these rhythms. Therefore, the transcriptions act as paradigms. By establishing a range of authenticity, they define the core elements of each salute and serve as performance models.

Mastering batá drumming is a huge undertaking and this book is not an exhaustive catalogue of batá rhythms. In fact, the salutes comprise just one part of the total repertoire. However, the salutes are the best place to begin the study of batá, for they are succinct, relatively easy to memorize, and encompass a wide range of rhythmic types. We strongly suggest that you stay within the bounds of proper style as outlined here until all of the material presented has been thoroughly grasped. First become a master of this particular style, then if you wish to further your understanding, continue with careful study of additional sources (see the discography and bibliography).

The salute rhythms are extracted from a drummed religious ceremony known as the *oru del igbodu.* Practitioners of Santería (known as Santeros or Santeras) believe the rhythms to be sonic representations of divine principles and assert that they are literally alive with the sacred potential embodied within the orichas that they represent. Because of this (as well as the confidential nature of Santería's rituals), we have chosen to present no music in this book that could not be heard by any non-Santero at an actual religious event, on a commercial recording, or at any one of the many folkloric performances which take place every year in both the Caribbean and the United States.

Batá drumming is a sacred art form which has served as a powerful voice for generations of Afro-Cuban musicians. It carries profound inner meaning to millions of religious practitioners throughout the New World. For the Santero, the salute rhythms speak with the voice of the gods. Play them with respect.

Finally, this book provides a map for musical performance, not ritual propriety. Santería is a religion shrouded in mystery, and there is no attempt made here to open that veil. Music is just one layer of ritual practice and all of the layers must work in harmony if the spiritual events that Santeros experience are to take place. If you truly want those experiences, go find an initiated Santero or Santera to be your teacher and guide. That kind of information is in no book.

John Amira and Steven Cornelius

Chapter Two

Historical Background

The origins of Santería are found within the traditional religion of the Yoruba peoples of West Africa. This chapter introduces basic religious conceptions, and provides a general overview of religious belief as it emerged from West Africa, to Cuba, and eventually to New York City.

As with the transcriptions, this undertaking is problematic because there is extensive variation in belief and custom at both micro and macro levels. For example, while a practitioner might provide a coherent and well formulated description of his or her own particular belief system, that system and the mythologies that support it tend to be constructed according to both personal and regional necessities. Quite simply, other practitioners will disagree. Not only is this true between large geographic areas (Yorubaland, Cuba and New York), but also between various temples within each area. Santeros reading this book may find that they have minor disagreements with some of the material discussed below. This cannot be helped. Because the music itself is the core of this book, our discussion of religious history and conception is limited. We have confined our overview to generally accepted ideas and take care to qualify the more controversial notions. (Our bibliography provides additional resources should you wish to further investigate religious doctrine.)

The Religious Context

Traditional Yoruba religion is constructed upon a hierarchical, pantheistic system of thought which stretches from God Almighty in the most rarified heaven to man on earth. Man can fulfill his destiny by avoiding the wrath of gods, and actually improve his lot through proper veneration and sacrifice to them.

Olorun is The Deity, God Almighty, and is generally considered to be responsible for the creation of the universe.[1] Olorun is an austere and remote God who by representing all things, all possibilities, is beyond human comprehension. Therefore, practitioners direct their entreaties to the orichas, deities who, positioned directly below Olorun, are both relatively fathomable and accessible.[2] Each oricha embodies various aspects from the totality of Olorun. These aspects are personified from natural features (rivers, oceans, mountains) or from elemental forces acting within nature (wind, lightning, disease). Through these associations, each oricha is believed to govern specific aspects of the universe. What evolves from these conceptions are layers of religious belief which reveal multiple notions of, and means to, the sacred.

Religious practitioners use music and various types of prayer to communicate with and praise the orichas. In turn, the orichas mediate between man and God Almighty. Direct contact with the orichas is sometimes achieved through spirit possession. This is an important aspect of worship in some areas of West Africa and central to New World music ritual.

Synthesis in Cuba

People of African heritage form nearly one third of the population of Cuba. Curtain (1969:46) estimates a total number of landed slaves at approximately 702,000, and of these, over 600,000 arrived as recently as the first sixty-five years of the 19th century. Among the major ethnic groups represented were the Yoruba.

The Cuban experience was generally hospitable to the oricha belief of the Yoruba, but the upheaval in location and social systems dictated the need for creative transformation and transmutation. Within slave society, because of ethnic diversity, beliefs and ritual customs were added or suspended to fit a new set of communal requirements.

An important influence was the Catholic Church. Importantly, because the church demanded at least some rights for the slaves, they were allowed to form their own social and religious organizations. Rather than try to destroy traditional beliefs, the church embraced a stance whereby within the Negro *cabildos* (social clubs), the traditional religion would be allowed to continue and gradually become influenced by Christian teachings. Membership within the cabildos followed regional African groupings called *naciones*, and members shared common ethnic and linguistic origins. Each cabildo was associated with a specific Catholic saint. In some cases the Africans noted the commonalities between the saints and the orichas and began to merge the concepts. In others, it appears that Africans simply found it expedient to camouflage the orichas as saints so that the church would not interfere with their true religious practices.

The following list describes the major attributes of the orichas and their syncretic match up/camouflage with Christianity. Each oricha has many avatars (called "roads" by Santeros) which manifest different characteristics. We present just some of each oricha's most common manifestations.

Eléggua — As the guardian of doors and crossroads, Eléggua is to be saluted first in order to open the way. In his various manifestations he is the messenger of the orichas, a guerrero or warrior deity, the controller of aché (divine potentiality), and a trickster. Santeros variously connect Eléggua with Saint Anthony, the child of Atocha, or Saint Roque.

Ogún — This is the warrior god of iron, war, and pure force. In Nigeria he is associated with oaths, and followers of the traditional belief system will kiss metal as a sign that they will tell the truth.[3] Santeros associate Ogún with Saint Peter.

Ochosi — Ochosi is the third warrior. He is the god of the hunt and is depicted by a bow and arrow. Ochosi hunts with Ogún and it is said that they are blood brothers. He is associated with Saint Norbert.

Obaloke — The king of the mountains. Beyond this, little is known, but according to Cabrera (1957:249) he is the defender of Obatalá. He is associated with Saint Robert.

Inle — A river oricha, Inle is worshipped by fishermen, and one might ask for his permission before going out onto the water. Inle is also associated with healing. He is syncretized with Saint Rafael.

Babalú Ayé — In Africa, Babalú Ayé is the oricha of smallpox and leprosy. Santeros in New York have recently been identifying him with diseases of the blood, and particularly with AIDS. He is an earth god and equalizes people rich or poor by punishing moral transgressions with disease. He is a "hot" and dangerous god who must be cooled frequently with water. Therefore, drummers will pour a bit of water on the floor before playing his salute rhythms. Babalú Ayé is associated with Saint Lazarus and is depicted as an old man on crutches.

Osain — Osain is the god of the forest, herbs and healing. He is physically diminished, with only one arm, one leg, and one eye — a price that he has paid for the selfishness of trying to hoard all of the forest's healing herbs. Osain is associated with Saint Sylvester and on occasion a variety of others, including: Saint Joseph and Saint Ramon.

Osun — Osun is the fourth warrior and a messenger of Obatalá. He is symbolized by an iron rooster and associated with the power of witchcraft. He is syncretized with John the Baptist or Saint Ismael.

Obatalá — Obatalá is the king of the orichas, the god of whiteness, justice, and purity. He created the world and is responsible for human existence. Different aspects of Obatalá are portrayed variously as an old man, a young man, and even a female. He is associated with Our Lady of Mercy, and is very popular in the New York area.

Dadá — A child of Obatalá and Yemayá, Dadá is considered to be either the older brother or sister of Changó. Dadá is associated with Our Lady of the Rosary.

Oggué — Little is known about Oggué. He is represented by the horns of a bull and is associated with Saint Blas.

Agayú — Agayú is generally considered to be the father of Changó. He is the power and principle of the volcano as it releases energy into the world. Agayú is associated with Saint Christopher.

Ibedyi — The Ibedyi are twin children of Changó and (according to various mythologies) either Oyá or Ochún. They are associated with Saints Cosmas and Damian.

Orula or Ifá — Orula is the god of divination and holds the secrets of destiny. His priests, known as babalawos, form a central part of the religious faith. He is syncretized with Saint Francis of Assisi.

Oricha Oko — Oricha Oko is an agriculture deity and associated with both the earth and fertility. He is syncretized with Saint Isidore.

Changó — Changó is both a deified ancestor and the god of lightning and thunder (considered by some to be the physical manifestation of divine illumination and retribution). Changó often carries his double headed thunder ax and loves the active quality of bright red. Not surprisingly, he is the most macho of the orichas and is known for his great virility. Curiously however, he is syncretized with the female Catholic saint — Saint Barbara (who is also associated with the color red and lightning). Changó is immensely popular in New York.

Yegguá — Yegguá is associated with the cemetery and is said to be very secretive, shy, and occasionally vain. Pure of heart, Yegguá is syncretized with The Virgin of Mount Serrate.

Oyá — By some accounts, a mistress of Changó, she is also associated with the wind. In her peaceful state, Oyá is a gentle breeze, but aroused she becomes a violent storm. Oyá is identified with the cemetery and the dead (egun). She is syncretized with either Our Lady of Candelaria or Saint Teresa.

Ochún — A river deity, Ochún is the goddess of love and beauty, and a favorite wife of Changó. Ochún is syncretized with Our Lady of Charity.

Yemayá — Yemayá is the symbol of motherhood and fertility. A river goddess in Africa, in the New World she has been transmuted into the power of the sea. Yemayá is associated with Our Lady of Regla.

Obba — A river goddess and jealous wife of Changó. She is syncretized with Saint Rita or Saint Catherine

Odudua — Odudua is credited amongst different myths as being both the creator of the earth and a deified ancestor who was once the leader of the Yoruba peoples. Odudua is syncretized with Saint Manuel.

The Foundations of Santería in New York City

The rhythms transcribed in this book can be heard throughout the New World. However, the authors' experience is most closely associated with the New York tradition and therefore we provide this additional background.

New York religious philosophy has numerous schisms which are at least partly due to the diversity in practitioners' ethnicity, social and economic backgrounds. There is a strong Latin community (Cuban and Puerto Rican) which generally maintains the religion as it is found in the Caribbean. However, there are also many African-Americans involved in the religion who are sometimes looking past Cuba and identifying with African ideals (Edwards and Mason 1985:V), and an increasing number of Anglo-Americans who have been attracted to Santería for a variety of other reasons.

Santería is relatively new to New York City. The religion was practiced privately by Cubans in the late 1940s, but it was probably not until the early 1960s that the first Americans were initiated in New York City. The religious community has grown dramatically from the late 1960s to the present. Amongst the most deeply involved practitioners, Santería entails a complete lifestyle in which the sacred and the secular are constantly interacting and influencing one another.

Transcription Sources — New York Tradition

The transcriptions that we are presenting in this book represent the dominant performance style of New York batá playing, which in turn grew out of the Havana batá style. While most of the basic rhythmic patterns are performed today in a manner that is very close to the rhythmic feel used in the 1960s, there is now a greater range of variation and interpretation than there once was. The reasons for both the similarity and expansion of style are easily identified. First, throughout the world, sacred music tends to be more resistant to change than does secular music. This is also the case for New York batá drumming where because of the sacred nature of the salute rhythms, personal creativity must follow the dictates of religious conception. The limits for change are defined by tradition (although the actual boundaries are hazy) and if a performer is seen as moving outside of these confines, the music can no longer be what it must.

Expansion of style follows the growing maturity of New York performance practice. What in the 1960s was a relatively unknown drumming style with few performers is now an established tradition. Today there are a number of experienced New York players from various backgrounds who perform in different batá styles. There is also more variation because the musical principles are better understood.

Batá drumming was introduced into the New York community by Cuban drummers in the late 1950s. While at that time there was already a strong Afro-Cuban presence in the commercial music business with such eminent drummers as Chano Pozo, Mongo Santamaria and Patato Valdez, New York ritual drumming finds its roots with Julio Collazo and Francisco Aguabella, perhaps the only people in the United States during the 1950s who understood the deeper intricacies of batá drumming.[4] In terms of New York tradition, Collazo is the most important, for Aguabella moved to the West Coast shortly after his arrival in the United States.

Before emigrating from Cuba, Collazo was a member of a batá ensemble headed by the legendary drummer, Pablo Roche.[5] When Collazo began to play ceremonies within the New York musical community, local drummers quickly became interested in learning how to perform. However, Collazo at first accepted no students and was generally reticent to share the bulk of his knowledge with outsiders, only on occasion demonstrating isolated rhythms. Therefore many musicians, after having been given a taste of the depth and beauty of batá drumming, were forced to go to non-conventional sources to learn the genre.

Traditionally, the technical and social requirements of ritual drumming for Santería are passed down directly from teacher to student. Apprentices learn the different drum parts in order beginning with the least complicated drum, the okónkolo. By performing in a group, the apprentice gradually learns the other parts, next mastering and performing on the itótele, and finally moving to the lead drum, the iyá.

With the exception of a very select group of musicians that Collazo eventually taught, the first New York drummers could not follow the traditional method. Instead, they used a combination of sources; watching and listening to the isolated examples that Collazo played, studying published transcriptions, and transcribing material from commercially available recorded examples.

The books of Cuban scholar Fernando Ortiz were very important in the early stages of New York batá performance. Ortiz published a number of volumes in the 1950s which provided a massive amount of general information about the music of Santería, including transcriptions of a major portion of the batá repertory. While the transcriptions are problematic, they provided insights into musical structure and therefore became an important source of information for New York musicians. Using the general map that the transcriptions provided, musicians then went to various sound recordings and began to work out the intricacies of batá drumming for themselves.[6]

Even at the beginning of the 1970s there were probably no more than three or four batá groups performing in the New York metropolitan area. However, in the mid-1970s interest boomed. Santería was becoming known to a broader cross-section of the population, and this was reflected in the attention that the music was receiving. Centered around specific rehearsal studios and energetic leaders, groups of musicians began to gather on a regular basis to learn the songs and play the rhythms.

The next stage in New York batá drumming began with the Mariel boat lift of 1980. Many of the arriving immigrants initially claimed (falsely) to be important and knowledgeable ritual drummers in Cuba. However, they were surprised to find an active, well established, and remarkably informed New York music scene. Therefore, of these new arrivals, only the best were able to maintain themselves within the musical community.

Clearly, the most influential of the Mariel immigrants has been Orlando Puntilla Rios, a recognized master drummer. With Puntilla's arrival, suddenly a virtuoso Cuban musician was on the scene who was more than willing to teach New York drummers the intricacies of batá and he quickly established himself as the primary source for information. Puntilla taught not only novices, but many of the more advanced New York drummers who went to him for confirmation and adjustments on material that they had already been playing for some years.

One of the major consequences of the Mariel immigration was a loosening up of performance style. New York musicians were suddenly confronted with a drumming style considerably less rigid than that which they themselves had come to play. No longer confined by relatively static sources of information (the Ortiz transcriptions and recordings), new innovations were assimilated into New York performance.

Musical and Religious Ideals

The process of gradual acculturation for New York drummers into the ideology of Santería is worth noting. New York drummers came to ritual performance from a variety of interests. However, after getting exposure to the religion, many drummers also developed a strong respect for Santería's religious beliefs. In fact, while most New York batá drummers are not Santeros, there seem to be very few who deny Santería's efficacy or potentialities.

When first learning to play, the musicians' considerations dealt primarily with issues relating to performance practice. However, with technical proficiency came opportunities to perform within a ritual context. The general consequence of this was a broadening in emphasis from purely technical matters to integrating religious ideology into performance. One example of this concerns the rules defining who may or may not play the drums. When New York musicians began learning and performing amongst themselves in the 1960s and 1970s, any musician who was tenacious enough could probably have gotten the opportunity to learn to play, for batá drumming was approached primarily in terms of musical knowledge rather than sacred formula. However, this situation began to change as the local musicians became more involved in liturgical performance. By playing for actual ceremonies drummers discovered a new range of possibilities. They learned to manipulate the musical and ritual factors under their control and thereby began to regulate the process of spirit possession. No longer was this just "drumming," rather, the music of the batá drums was once again sounding its highest potential — it was invoking the orichas. This direct confrontation and integration of the music with the sacred broadened the musicians' overall perspective from a sonic focus to a view more in line with Santería's cosmology.

The movement towards a philosophical basis for music making had an insular effect on the performance scene. For example, because of issues dealing with sexuality, many New York musicians consider it taboo for the batá drums to be played by either women or homosexual men. Initially, because their interest was focused on aural constructs rather than religious ideology, the musicians ignored these restrictions. Today however, many drummers that regularly perform in ritual settings accept these values and carry them to the rest of their batá performance relationships. Consequently, because instruction is denied to some, teaching that briefly took place in institutionalized settings is no longer possible.[7]

Footnotes

1. He is also sometimes called by the names *Olodumare* or *Olofi.* Some New York practitioners consider them to be separate and unrelated entites, while still others believe that the three orichas form the holy trinity.
2. Idowu (1962:60) believes oricha to come from the Yoruba word *orise,* which means "headsource." *Ori* means the physical head but more importantly, it is "the essence of personality, the ego." If *se* is the correct ending patern, then the word implies "the source of *ori,*" i.e., God Almighty.
3. See Sandra Barnes' *Ogún: An Old God for a New Age* for a fascinating description of Ogún in contemporary Yoruba society.
4. Both musicians came over at the request of Katherine Dunham and it seems likely that the first batá drumming to be widely heard in the United States was done in this secular context.
5. Roche is particularly important in this history because he provided major assistance to the Cuban scholar Fernando Ortiz, who was the first to attempt a systematic cataloging and transcription of batá rhythms.
6. The most influential recording was published on the Orfeon label. It was "Afro Tambores Batá" (Orfeon LP-LAB-08). The batá ensemble was headed by Giraldo Rodriguez. Jesús Pérez, a student and member of Pablo Roche's ensemble, also performed with this group and was probably playing iyá on at least some if not all of the tracks.
7. Interestingly enough, in present day Cuba members of the Conjunto Folklorico Nacional and other individuals teach batá openly to anyone, regardless of sex or sexual preference. In Nigeria as well, women are sometimes taught to play. Omibiyi (1975:503) tells of a batá player who taught his daughters to play when he failed to have male children.

Chapter Three

The Instrumental Ensemble

Batá are double headed, hourglass shaped drums, generally considered to be "owned" by the oricha Changó. (The shape is said to represent Changó's thunder axe.) On each drum, the larger drumhead is called the *enú* (mouth) and the smaller higher pitched head is called the *chachá* (butt). Both heads are sounded with the hands.

Construction

The batá ensemble is made up of three drums: *iyá* (mother drum), *itótele* (or *omelé enkó*), and *okónkolo* (or simply, *omelé*). Iyá, the largest and lowest pitched drum, is the lead instrument in the ensemble. It is assigned the most complicated rhythms and has the most freedom for embellishment. Itótele is the middle sized drum. It engages in occasional variation as well as regular conversation with the iyá. Okónkolo, the smallest drum, is generally confined to rhythmic ostinatos.

It should be noted that there are two types of batá; *aberikula* and *aña*. Aberikula (unbaptized) drums may be played by anyone. Drums with aña (fundamento or baptized drums) may only be played by people who have gone through a special initiation.

Because the batá drum is a symbol of unity, the shell should ideally be constructed by hollowing out a single piece of wood. However, using wooden slat construction is much simpler and this is how most American drums are assembled. There are also instruments available which have been made from molded fiberglass. While fiberglass tends to be louder, most batá drummers prefer the deeper tones of wooden drums.[1]

Traditionally, the skins are set on hoops and then suspended upon the drum. The drumheads are then tensioned by rope (or leather thongs) which are interlaced from one hoop, along the body of the instrument to the other hoop. The rope is held taut by wrapping and interlacing it along the shell of the drum body. Some drummers

Photograph 3.1 — Batá drums – traditionally strung set

believe that a direct benefit from the traditional method is that the tension of both heads becomes interrelated.

Today, most drums that are commercially available use metal tuning lugs. While this method is certainly more convenient, it is only feasible for aberikula drums. Because fundamento batá are believed to be the embodiment of active sacred principles, they must be constructed from materials that were once living (wood, skin, rope). Second, while this idea is not universally accepted, some Santeros believe that Changó's drums should not be constructed from products made of Ogún's metal, iron. Ogún and Changó are considered enemies by many New York Santeros and mixing these ideas within a ritual context may confuse and weaken a ceremony's potency.

The iyá is decorated with strands of brass bells (*tchaworo*) which are strung around the shell along the heads. These bells are sometimes associated with Ochún (one of Changó's many wives) but authorities disagree on this point. The tchaworo sweeten the percussive sound of the iyá by ringing whenever the drum is struck. In some situations the iyá player may choose to sound the tchaworo by shaking the drum rather than striking the heads.

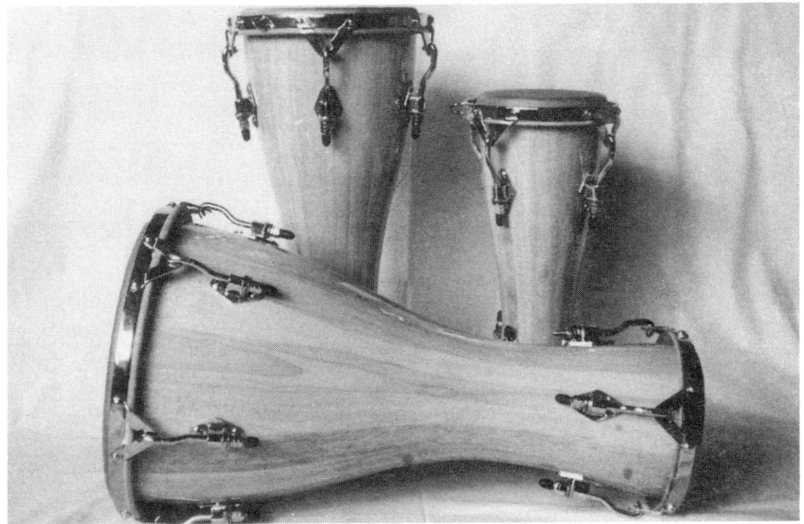

Photograph by John Amira

Photograph 3.2 — Batá drums – modern tunable set

The shells and skins of batá drums are never marked with religious symbols. However, the drums are generally dressed in a decorated (loin) cloth called a *bante* (Thompson [1983:95-6] provides a detailed description of these religious garments).

Tuning

Each individual performance differs in terms of absolute pitch range according to where individual drums sound best, how the drums sound in relationship to each other, and problems relating to skin heads reacting to changes in humidity. Although there is no ideal pitch that each skin should be tuned to, there is an ideal pitch relationship within the ensemble. The enú of the okónkolo should be identical in pitch with the chachá of the itótele. Likewise, the enú of the itótele should be identical with the chachá of the iyá.

Generally speaking, the objective when tuning drums with tension chords is to get them as high as possible, because it is extremely difficult to get sufficient tension when working with materials such as rope or rawhide. Furthermore, once you begin to play, the drums will start to lose some of their tautness. However, when tuning lug drums one should be careful to not tune the drums too tightly because there is a point beyond which the drums will no longer resonate freely.

One final aspect of tuning must be mentioned. The iyá should have a ring of clay called *idá* or *fardela* molded onto the enú head. The idá works to darken the drum's timbre by dampening overtones and lowering the pitch. A simple recipe for making the idá is as follows: mix together 2 lbs. reddish clay, 2 oz. castor oil, and 2 tbs. rosin.[2]

Symbolism

Conceptions about the batá drums are immersed in a wealth of mythological ideals which relate to the embodiment and transference of sacred power. We believe that familiarity with some of these concepts is essential for having a sense of what it means to play batá. As with previous discussions, some ideas seem to conflict. Ultimately however, all of the levels speak to the common goal of religious efficacy.

Male/female polarities and kinship relations are essential to batá symbolism. The batá set is considered to be a family of drums led by the iyá or mother drum. The drummers are a part of this family. They serve the batá and are known as *omóaña* — "children of the god of the drums."[3]

The drummers also form a fraternity amongst themselves. In traditional performance, there is a hierarchical relationship of elders and novices in which the master drummer leads the ensemble from the iyá, while the second and third ranking persons play the itótele and okónkolo respectively. This sense of fraternity goes well beyond one's specific ensemble. Proficiency on batá serves as a badge of musical and cultural accomplishment and is highly respected by musicians and Santeros alike.

Another interpretation of the drummers' relationship with the batá also supports the idea of unity through kinship. Rather than children of the drums, some musicians refer to themselves as married to the drums. The "child" of this marriage is the dynamic sounding of sacred rhythmic potential.

The batá drums are one of the many voices of the orichas. They represent the embodiment of power and musicians provide the key to activation. Because of this, drummers are highly respected within the religious community. They speak the sacred language of the orichas, coaxing or occasionally tricking them into making an appearance.

Footnotes

1. There are a number of companies manufacturing batá drums today. The drums pictured above were made by Latin Percussion according to John Amira's specifications.
2. Ortiz (1952:265-266) gives additional recipes which use plants and other materials specifically native to Cuba.
3. The iyá player is sometimes known as the *olu batá* or chief of the drums. It is a title of honor and few New York drummers consider their knowledge full enough to merit such a title.

Chapter Four

Musical Structure

There are two main types of public music ceremonies in Santería. One, called *bembé* (or "drum and güiro" after the instrumental combination), is performed using conga drums, *agbés* (also called güiros), and an iron bell. The other ceremonial type, formally called *güemilere*, is with batá drums and sometimes a small rattle called an acheré. However, in New York it is equally common to hear the güemilere referred to as a bembé, *tambor* (drum), or *toque* (a rhythm or beat). Of these two ensemble types, batá drumming is more structured, complex, and generally considered more sacred than the drum and güiro style.

The Music Ceremonies

Bembés and/or güemileres honor the orichas, and may be held for a variety of specific reasons, including: to celebrate the sacred day of an oricha, to celebrate the anniversary of an individual's initiation into Santería (often called a birthday party), to honor the oricha of one's elder in the religion, to express gratitude to an oricha for a special benefaction that has already been granted, or to tribute the oricha in anticipation of some future benevolence.

Public music ceremonies have a number of distinct sections. If batá drums are used, the first section is the *oru del igbodu* (lit., "ceremony in the oricha's room," it is also called the *oru seco* — unadorned oru). The oru del igbodu occurs prior to the general social activities of the güemilere and although a few people may come into the performance area to listen, it is drummed in relative seclusion before an altar that has been specially constructed for the oricha being honored at that particular ceremony. Because the salutes are played directly to the orichas some drummers consider this to be the most important part of a music ceremony.

The second section of the güemilere is the *oru del eyá aranla* (lit., "ceremony in the main room," it is also called the *oru cantado* — sung oru).[1] The oru del eyá aranla (and the rest of the ceremony) is led by a singer who engages those in attendance with songs in a call and response style. The performance now takes place in a large room and begins after much of the general public has arrived. Once again, like the oru del igbodu, the oru del eya aranla honors the various orichas, but this time it simultaneously honors each Santero by having him come forward and dance when the music for his oricha is being played. It is important to note that the batá rhythms for this section are sometimes, but not always, the same as those in the oru del igbodu. If the ceremony is in the drum and güiro style, the rhythms played are generic and acceptable for any of the orichas.

The music ceremony moves without break from the oru del eyá aranla to the next section, the *iban balo* (lit., "patio"). In terms of formal structure, the iban balo is much more free than either of the preceding sections. While the oricha of honor may get much of the musical attention, the singer controls the musical flow and will generally move the ceremony along lines that receive the most interest and participation (singing and dancing) from those in attendance. The iban balo is the section in which spirit possession is most likely to occur.

The final section of the bembé or tambor is the *cierre* or closing. Salute rhythms are played to the *egun* (spirits of the ancestors) and the following orichas: Oyá, Babalú Ayé, Osain, Yegguá, Yemayá, Eléggua, and Olokun. The cierre is similar to the oru del igbodu (except for the final closing songs to Eléggua and Olokun) in that both sections are primarily instrumental only, salute rhythms are played and the drumming is addressed directly to the orichas, and each section acts as a marker — the oru del igbodu brings the ceremony into sacred time and space while the cierre provides an exit.

The Oru del Igbodu

The oru del igbodu is designed to honor the orichas, and takes 20 to 30 minutes to perform. While there are no songs that accompany the drumming, it is believed that the batá drums themselves are speaking. They speak on two levels: first, metaphorically, by imitating in sound the spiritual nature of each of the orichas, and second, in a concrete fashion by reciting musical phrases which are actual representations on the drums of Yoruba speech inflections. Ortiz (1965:376) relates these phrases to a style of Yoruba praise poetry called *oríki.* All of the salute rhythms have a number of distinct musical sections (called "roads" by the Santeros), some of which were derived from oríki. In New York (and Cuba), much of the linguistic information is lost, but each road is believed to be a sonic representation of a different avatar of the oricha.

The oru del igbodu systematically honors and invokes the blessings of each oricha worshipped within the Santería pantheon. The salutes begin with rhythms for Eléggua, the oricha of the crossroads who opens the doors to all possibilities. The series ends with a salute to the particular oricha that is being specially honored in the ceremony, followed by Odudua. Most ensembles place the salute rhythms in the following order: Eléggua, Ogún, Ochosi, Obaloke, Inle, Babalú Ayé, Osain, Osun, Obatalá, Dadá, Oggué, Agayú, Orula or Ifa, Oricha Oko, Ibedyi, Changó, Yegguá, Oyá, Ochún, Yemayá, Obba, Odudua.[2]

None of the individual rhythms from the oru del igbodu take more than three or four minutes to perform and some may be as short as one minute. Generally, the length depends on the amount of musical material to be presented, but also varies with individual preferences.

The Concept of Clave

At the root of all batá rhythms lies a concept called clave. Clave is a Spanish word which translates as clef, key, or keystone. In Cuban musical terminology it means either a pair of sticks for playing rhythms, the specific patterns played, or the underlying rules which govern these patterns. This last definition is the one that concerns us. It is somewhat analogous to the image of the keystone—the wedge shaped stone placed at the top of an arch which locks all the other stones in place.

Clave is a two measure pattern in which each measure is diametrically opposed. The two measures are not at odds, but rather, they are balanced opposites like positive and negative, expansive and contractive, or the poles of a magnet. As the pattern is repeated, an alternation from one polarity to the other takes place creating pulse and rhythmic drive. Were the pattern to be suddenly reversed, the rhythm would be destroyed as in a reversing of one magnet within a series.

Figure 4.1 - The Clave

The examples above show two (of many) possible clave patterns in both 4/4 and 6/8 time. In each case the first measure is positive and expansive while the second measure is negative and contractive.

In batá drumming the patterns are held in place according to both the internal relationships between the drums and their relationship with clave. This double fit is a natural and integral part of the batá rhythms. Study will show that the rhythms themselves, in mirroring clave, have their own positive and negative sides. Should the drums fall out of clave (and in contemporary practice they sometimes do) the internal momentum of the rhythm will be dissipated and perhaps even broken. This aspect will take on considerable importance when considering proper performance style in Chapter Five.

The Salutes

There are four fundamental structural levels within each salute rhythm: *llames* (calls), roads (some of which are derived from oríki, all of which serve primarily as musical sections today), *conversaciónes* (conversations), and variations.[3] The central level is the road, which we identify as "sections" in our transcriptions. Each section is a complete and distinct musical phrase. While some salutes have only one section, a few have more than six. Although the rhythmic patterns within sections may vary slightly from ensemble to ensemble, the distinctive motivic ideas are always similar and musicians from one ensemble can readily identify the salutes of another.

When there are differences in the section patterns used by each ensemble, the greatest deviation will be found within the iyá part. In contrast, sectional rhythmic patterns between ensembles are most similar for the okónkolo parts, where the level of freedom for embellishment is lowest.

The second fundamental structural level is the call (or llame). In the salute rhythms, calls are always sounded by the iyá player. There are three types of calls. The first type is an entrance call. It identifies and initiates the salute rhythm to be played. When sounded, the itótele and okónkolo players are expected to recognize the salute and enter at the correct place within the rhythmic pattern.

The second type of call moves the ensemble from one section to the next. In order to be recognized as such by the other drummers, iyá must sound the section change at the proper place within the rhythmic framework, otherwise it will be misinterpreted as mere embellishment and ignored. When the change is correctly signaled, itótele and okónkolo must shift to the rhythms of the new section.

Finally, there are calls for conversation. Conversation takes place between iyá and itótele and always stays within a single section. Like calls for section changes, they must be sounded and responded to at the correct place within the rhythmic structure.[4]

The transcriptions reveal how the iyá leads the ensemble through the salutes. Each basic section pattern highlights and opens up the door to a fixed set of musical information, and there are established progressions which the drummers must follow as they move from one rhythmic section to the next. Musical commands must be nested within the proper context or they will not be understood. Within every salute there are many detours which may be taken to lead away from the section's basic rhythmic pattern into variations or conversations, but the ensemble can only move to the next section through context- specific rhythmic doors. In most cases, variations and conversations must return to the standard pattern motives that generated them before the call to change sections may be given.

Ensemble Performance

Playing batá is a group undertaking. While any of the rhythms, for any of the drums, may be relatively easy to perform by itself, this is often not the case when performing within the ensemble. Each drum has its own specific rhythmic identity, but when combined in ensemble performance the various parts interlock to create what may be an entirely different rhythmic sensation for each of the musicians. In fact, in the early stages of learning it is not uncommon to lose track of the very sounds that one creates on his own drum amongst the broader sounds of the ensemble. While disconcerting at first, this may also be a positive sign, for it suggests that one's ears are experiencing and assimilating the totality of the ensemble rather than being locked onto a single musical line.

If you are starting an ensemble with equally experienced drummers and beginning your batá studies with this book, taking an egalitarian approach is probably best. The ensemble effect of batá rhythms sounds very different depending on the perspective from which you listen. Therefore, trade off drums and learn all three parts. It will take longer for your group to be able to perform all of the transcriptions, but achieving the ability to hear the ensemble while performing on any of the drums will help you to assimilate the essence of each particular rhythm more thoroughly.

An excellent way to develop your sense of ensemble while practicing alone is to sing one drum part (or the clave) while playing another. This is difficult and sometimes frustrating but it strengthens musical time and aural skills. Begin with the easiest combination — playing okónkolo while singing the clave (and visa versa). Gradually learn to play the other drums with the clave, then combine the singing and playing of drum lines.

Instrumental Roles

Each drum has its own particular ensemble function and idiomatic rhythmic structures. The okónkolo is the time keeper and the rhythmic anchor for the ensemble. Of the three drums, its rhythms are the least complex and the most stable. In general, the okónkolo rhythms sound on the main metric pulses, have the shortest cycles, and show the least amount of variation. Because the position is relatively undemanding, playing in the okónkolo chair provides an excellent opportunity to learn to hear the complex interlocking rhythms of batá.

Itótele is the work horse, the energizing force. Its rhythms are more complex than those for okónkolo, tend to span longer cycles, and most importantly, fill the unstable space between the metric pulses. As with okónkolo, the itótele player must understand iyá calls for beginnings, endings and section changes. However, itótele must also recognize and respond to calls for conversation. Because of the density of subtle variation which is sounded by iyá, the itótele player must be constantly interpreting iyá's performance, discerning between those calls which demand response versus simple embellishment. The itótele response to iyá must be immediate and exact in order to fit into the proper rhythmic frame. The itótele player should work to reach the point where his response to iyá calls is completely automatic and natural — just like speech. Batá drummers often make a game out of this musical dialogue, with iyá constantly testing itótele's ability to answer correctly.

Iyá rhythmic patterns are longer and more complex than those for okónkolo or itótele; within the constraints of proper style, the iyá player is relatively free to vary the level of rhythmic embellishment and intensity. The iyá player is responsible for the big picture. He must creatively build his performance from correct musical standards while simultaneously guiding the ensemble through the maze of rhythmic complexities. This can be a difficult task and requires considerable musical sensitivity. Too much embellishment will take away from the power of the standard pattern and may even confuse the ensemble, while too little embellishment will make for an uninteresting performance. In a ritual context this balance is even more difficult to achieve, for there the iyá player is expected to use all of the aesthetic forces at his disposal to invoke the sacred by calling, praising and appeasing the gods.

Playing Technique

The traditional setup for the batá ensemble places the iyá in the middle. Itótele sets up to the iyá's left and okónkolo to iyá's right. The lower pitched head, the enu, is sounded by the player's right hand and the chachá is played with the left hand. (Left handed players sometimes reverse this.)

The sound produced on the chachá is always a staccato slap. It is generated by striking the drum head with the three outside fingers.

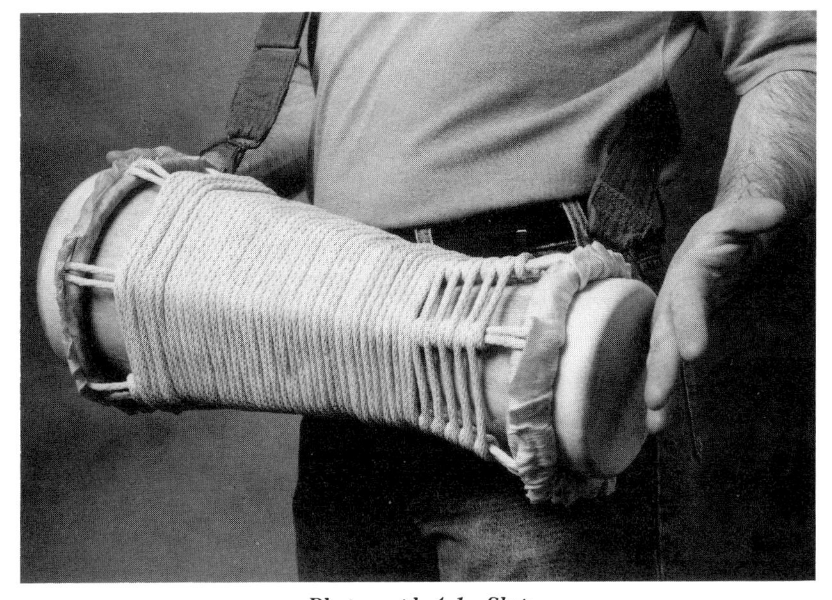

Photograph 4.1 - Slap

Photograph 4.2 - Okónkolo muff

Photograph 4.3 - Okónkolo tone

Photograph 4.4 - Itótele muff

Photograph 4.5 - Iyá muff

Photograph 4.6 - Itótele tone

Photograph 4.7 - Iyá tone

Photograph 4.8 - Enú touch

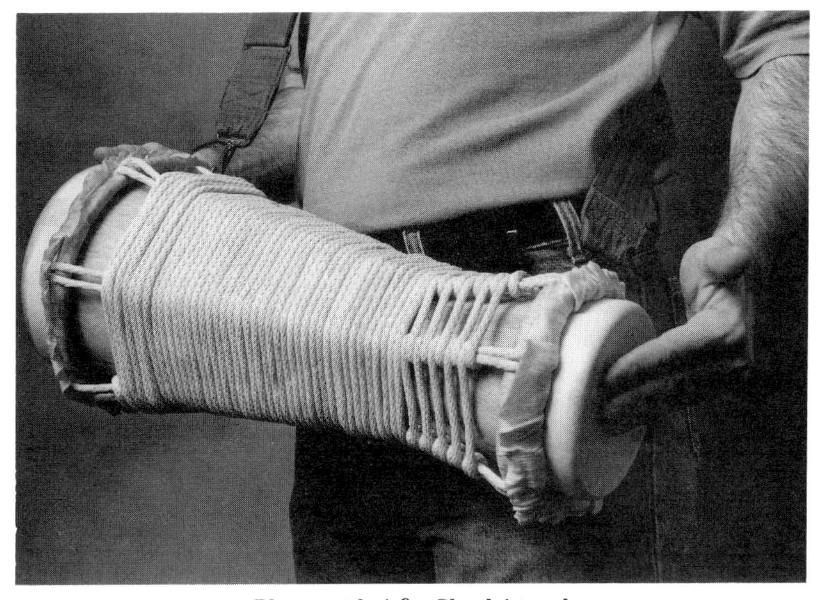

Photograph 4.9 - Chachá touch

The force is achieved mostly through a quick twisting motion of the wrist and forearm, although movement from the elbow and shoulder are necessary for loud playing. Upon striking, the performer's fingers disengage from the drum head while the outside corner of the palm presses on the skin to achieve a balance between a dry slap and a ringing tone.

There are two important techniques for striking the enú head: open (resonant) and closed (muffled) sounds. The closed stroke is sounded by striking the drum head with the flat of the hand and holding the hand against the head to stop the vibration. Depending on hand size, this effect might be achieved on the smaller drums (the itótele and okónkolo) by using just the four fingers. However, on the iyá one might find it necessary to use the palm as well as the fingers.

The open stroke is also sounded differently on each of the drums. Okónkolo may produce a good quality open or muffled tone through striking the drum so that the rim lies between the first and second joints of the fingers. For itótele, the rim should lie along the line that separates the fingers from the palm. The iyá stroke is produced by forming the hand into a shallow cup and striking the drum with the full hand between the rim and the idá. Iyá muffled tones are done by pressing the first two joints of the fingers down near the middle of the head.

Finally, we have included touch strokes. They are used for timing only and are not audible. Nevertheless, touches form an important part of batá performance by helping the performer to internalize and lock into the proper rhythmic groove. Think of batá drumming as a dance for the hands. Touches constitute those subtle weight shifts between steps, the balance points where the dancer must choose and define his next movements. When studying the transcriptions notice that most touches anticipate the movement from one drumhead to the other, a right hand touch will be followed by a left hand stroke and visa versa.

Touches need not be played, nor are the ones transcribed the only possibilities. However, they can be very helpful, so use our recommendations until you are thoroughly familiar with the rhythms. Then, if you wish to delete or modify them, go ahead. Careful listening to the recordings listed in the discography will be instructive. Some touches that we suggest for iyá become sounded notes within other ensembles. (And vice versa, others may play some of our sounded notes as touches.) This is natural, for touches are placed at rhythmic pressure points which often serve as the basis for variation and conversation.

Touches are played by bringing the tips of all four fingers gently against the drumhead. In general, they should be mentally and physically grouped to feel like either a response to the preceding slap or a timing setup for an upcoming stroke. With a little practice you will find that the touch is a natural extension of normal performance.

Footnotes

1. If the ceremony is a drum and güiro bembé, the oru del eya aranla is the opening section.
2. Ortiz (1965:379-80) lists Ibedyi before Oricha Oko.
3. Ortiz (1965) transcribes only calls and roads.
4. There is one exception in the Ogún salute where itótele calls the conversation.

Chapter Five

Transcription and Analysis

Any method of transcription is inherently problematic in rendering a musical style true to its actual sound. This is particularly so when using European methods to represent an African-Atlantic tradition. Nevertheless, we have decided that staff notation, while flawed, is the best method for presenting batá rhythms to a general audience. However, despite being portrayed as accurately as possible, the transcriptions alone will sometimes not be able to capture the ideal rhythmic flow. Metric sense can be very elusive and sometimes the rhythms fall between the "cracks," that is, they are neither truly duple nor triple in feel.[1] To achieve mastery, it will be necessary to do careful stylistic listening to authentic performances or, even better, study and perform with an accomplished batá player.

Transcription Problems

While we have assigned meters to the examples, the reader should avoid the traditional implications of metric accents. The rhythms are generally felt in two beats per measure, but performers should also be aware of metric weight derived from the implicit clave cycles that we have provided with the iyá call for each salute.

In the transcriptions that follow, the drums are arranged according to pitch: okónkolo on top, itótele in the middle, and iyá on the bottom. Clave is presented in the opening system only, but (with the exception of Inle) should be considered to extend throughout the salute.

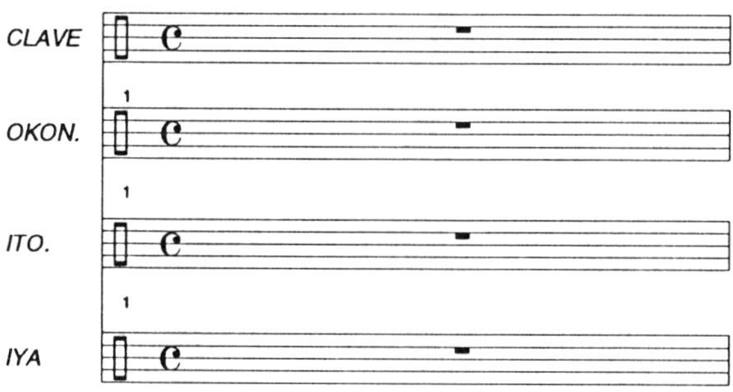

Figure 5.1 - Transcription arrangement.

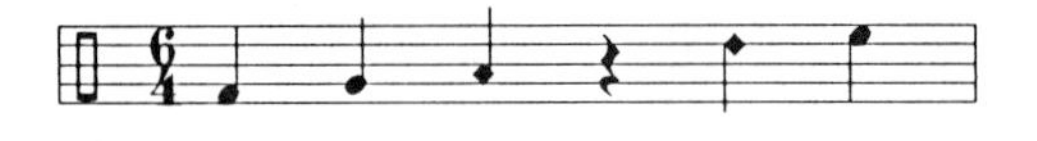

Figure 5.2 - Open enú tone, closed enú tone, enú touch, chachá touch, chachá slap

We have transcribed every score with four bars to the line so that clave can easily be superimposed over any musical segment. Each drum is transcribed on a single staff. The two strokes for the higher pitched chachá head (touch and slap) are indicated above the three lower pitched enú strokes (open, closed, touch). In order to facilitate reading the touch strokes have been given diamond shaped noteheads. The closed enú stroke is slightly higher in pitch than the open stroke and has therefore been placed on the line above the open stroke space. In Figure 1 the enú and chachá strokes (separated by a rest) are shown in the following order: open enú tone, closed enú tone, enú touch, chachá touch, chachá slap.

Finally, a few words about correctly following the road map through our transcriptions. We have set off all sections with repeat signs, and at the discretion of the iyá player, sections might be repeated once or many times. Variations and conversations are set off by heavy bar lines only. However, they too are sometimes repeated in performance. It is also not unusual for an ensemble to play a variation or conversation, return to the standard section pattern and then go back to play that same variation or conversation again. In general, there is no set formula for these things and when appropriate we have left this aspect of the transcriptions as open as possible. Perhaps the best rules to follow come from logical, musical sense. If the rhythm is played too long it will become uninteresting. If it goes by too quickly it will not feel well centered for either the ensemble or the listener. The very process of learning how to play the rhythms will give you a sense of these ideas. Further insights will be gleaned by listening to examples listed in the discography.

In order to keep the transcriptions unmuddled, we have made our designations for musical segments as concise as possible. Variations and conversations are identified first by their section affiliation and then by their order within that section. Following this procedure, Variation 1-A is the first variation within Section 1 and Conversation 3-B is the second conversation within Section 3.

Eléggua

The entrance, which is played one time, establishes the tempo and brings the ensemble into Section 1. After playing Section 1 for several repetitions, variations and conversations may be called at the iyá's discretion. In general, after each variation or conversation the ensemble will return to the basic pattern for several repetitions. However, on occasion variations and/or conversations may be played back to back. After a suitable length of time (perhaps 60 seconds) the iyá will call Section 2.

The iyá pattern in the Entrance to Section 2 is exactly the same as the Section 1 pattern except that the final muffled stroke is deleted. This stroke is left off for convenience so that the iyá double stroke downbeat of Section 2 (slap and tone) can be sounded cleanly. However, from a structural perspective the deletion is not necessary. Because the itótele does not change its pattern until the second half of the Section 2 cycle, the change in the iyá's pattern at the beginning of the section gives the itótele an entire measure to adjust.

In the Entrance to Section 3 a distinct iyá call occurs prior to the new section proper. When this happens the ensemble can change simultaneously at the beginning of the new section. This entrance also provides a good example of how correct musical performance depends on the proper interpretation of nested commands. Notice that the iyá pattern combines motives from Section 2 and Conversation 1-A. However, in this case because of the context in which the "Conversation 1-A" pattern is sounded, it must be interpreted as a call to Section 3.

The Entrance to Section 4 demonstrates a third method for enacting a section change. In this case the Section 4 iyá pattern itself serves as the call. However, because the itótele pattern is different from the downbeat, one measure is needed in order to completely adjust to the new pattern.

The Call to Section 5 works like the Call to Section 3, occurring before the section proper. Each of these last four sections should be played for approximately 30 seconds.

This final section is generally closed at the end of the third clave. The iyá may signal the end by either playing a series of alternating open and muffled tones, or by interjecting the call for the salute rhythms to Ogún.

Ogún

Some New York Santeros relate the rhythmic power of Ogún's duple meter angular salute to the sound of the oricha shaping iron at his forge or an army marching. These analogies are particularly appropriate for the patterns in Section 1 where staccato slap strokes dominate the overall sound. In almost every other salute the slaps between okónkolo and itótele are distributed across beats in order to fill sonic space and create rhythmic flow, but in Ogún's salute the instruments double their slap strokes, creating a driving quality to the rhythm which is even further enhanced by the iyá slap which begins each two measure phrase.

There is a brief melodic motive sounded between the tenor and bass open strokes of the itótele and iyá. The syncopated iyá open stroke is highly active and works to offset the centering quality of the okónkolo and itótele slap strokes. Itótele's following open stroke (which corresponds to the last note in the clave cycle) resolves the iyá syncopation by landing the brief open tone melody back on a main pulse.

The variations in Section 1 provide rhythmic contrast. Musicians might choose to play either one or both of them in performance. (It is also possible that some ensembles would play either of the variations as their main pattern.) If played as variations, they are to be played a few times only and then the iyá should return to the basic pattern.

From the Transition to Entrance the iyá may go to either the Optional Entrance Call (which can be repeated several times) or to the Section 2 entrance proper (which would be played one time). The call for the Conversation preceding Conversation 2-A is also optional.

It is common for ensembles to go back and forth between Sections 1 and 2 in the Ogún salute. After the initial playing of Section 1 iyá may choose patterns from either Section 1 or 1-B.

Ogún may be ended from either section, although it is most common for the iyá to signal the end (with the usual muffled strokes or by calling Ochosi) from Section 2.

Ochosi

Section 1 of the Ochosi salute is unusual in that despite the fact that the iyá pattern is only one measure long, the ensemble pattern lasts four measures (two clave cycles). The reason for this is that an itótele variation occurs at the beginning of the second clave cycle (measures 3 and 7 respectively). In fact, there is some disagreement about this figure. Some New York ensembles [and Ortiz (1965:379)] place the variation at the point that we have transcribed while many New York groups put it at the end of the second clave cycle (i.e., measures 4 and 8). We have chosen to follow the older authority of the Ortiz example in our transcription, but current practice favors the second interpretation.[2]

Whether an ensemble places the itótele variation in measures 3/7 or 4/8, iyá must call the entrances to Sections 2 and 3 from the proper point within the larger cycle. This means that iyá must be aware of both the itótele variations and the unsounded clave.

Section 3 presents one of the most difficult duple meter patterns for the itótele. Played alone, the off beat slaps tend to drag below the tempo required. Therefore, the touches become essential reference points for centering the rhythm. Initially, there may be a temptation to play the touches on the main pulses or between every slap, but we do not recommend this. Playing them as transcribed adds the correct idiomatic swing to the rhythm.

With the Entrance to Section 7 the tempo picks up a bit. As this happens the rhythmic feel relaxes and is rounded towards a triple meter. The Ochosi salute ends with a constant acceleration of Section 8. When the tempo becomes unplayable, iyá calls the end with open and muffled strokes.

Obaloke

The form of Obaloke is quite straight forward and requires little explanation. You may freely move back and forth between Sections 1 and 2. Obaloke ends on the downbeat of either section, but a Section 1 ending is generally preferred.

While structurally uncomplicated, Obaloke does present some technical difficulties. First, the slap strokes interlock between all three drums in Section 1. This creates a running staccato melody which must be balanced in terms of rhythmic feel and dynamics, and requires ensemble practice to maintain. Second, Obaloke is the first of the triple meter salutes to be played at a moderately fast tempo. As tempo increases, the syncopation between slap strokes becomes more difficult to maintain (especially for itótele.) Solving these problems in Obaloke is essential to being able to perform many of the later salutes.

Inle

The rhythms for Inle are straightforward, and due in part to the fact that itótele tends to mirror iyá's patterns throughout, the salute has a very grounded, stable feeling.

However, there is one significant complication, for there are two versions of Section 5. Version 1 (m.17) may raise some eyebrows amongst accomplished players, for it represents an older form which probably has been rarely heard since the 1950s. We place it first because it adheres to clave. Alternate Section 5 portrays the rhythm as it is generally played today. We have changed the meter in order to accommodate the seven beat patterns in the iyá and itótele. Meanwhile the okónkolo retains its earlier structure. This means that the iyá and itótele patterns must be repeated four times before realigning with the okónkolo cycle.

We do not know how the separation in styles occurred. Both rhythms seem to have existed simultaneously for many years. According to some, the batá drums in duplicating language are not obliged to follow a clave since everyday speech does not. However, that rings false to us, for if that were truly the case, then the majority of the rhythms that we present would show the same irregularities. Therefore, rather than view this whole process in terms of language, it seems more appropriate to see this particular aberration as an evolution based on musical rather than lexical grounds.

Inle ends on the last iyá tone of the Section 5 pattern.

Babalú Ayé

Babalú Ayé is the leveler of social inequities and bringer of "moral retribution" (Thompson 1983:62). He is greatly feared, easily angered, and difficult to appease once aroused. He is a "hot" oricha and believed to be most powerful in the heat of mid-day. Therefore, when playing the oru del igbodu it is common for drummers to "cool" the god by sprinkling some water on the ground prior to playing his salutes.

Babalú Ayé has two salutes, neither of which is complicated. In the first salute it is important to repeat the full iyá pattern. (Notice that measures 3-4, 5-6, and 9-10 are identical). In the second salute it is common for the second of the consecutive iyá slaps in measures 4, 8, 12 and 16, 20, 24 to be slightly delayed. This provides tension by giving the illusion that the tempo is slowing down. (It should not.)

The transcription of Section 1 in the second salute appears to be lacking an iyá entrance pattern. Because Section 1 is some six claves long, rather than transcribe Section 1 twice, we filled in the itótele and okónkolo parts immediately from the beginning. The actual iyá call is simply the pattern in the first measure (usually preceded by a muffled stroke sixteenth note upbeat). When the entrance is called the other drums enter as quickly as possible. The itótele should enter with the double stop eighth notes of measure one. Okónkolo should enter with the upbeat to measure two.

The first salute ends with the iyá slap stroke on the downbeat of the second half of the fourth clave of Section 1. The second salute ends on the last iyá slap at the end of Section I or Conversation 1-A.

Osain

Section 1 is often difficult for an ensemble to master. As in Obaloke, the problem is in setting up the interlocking slaps between all three drums (especially mms. 5 and 6). The okónkolo player in particular must be firm in centering his concentration on his open tones. Focusing on the slaps will cause the rhythm to suddenly appear displaced against the other drums.

The Entrance to Section 2 may be played after the Section 1 pattern or either of the conversations. In the switch to Section 2 the pulse remains the same — the new half note equals the old dotted quarter note. Itótele can be important in solidifying this change because it has been sounding the duple division throughout Section 1 (mms. 4-6, 8-10, 12-14, and 16-18).

Osain ends on the downbeat of Section 4.

Osun

Although we left it out of the transcription, the iyá call to open Osun often begins with an open tone sixteenth note upbeat. This stroke is a natural extension of the Section 1 pattern.

Here we encounter a problem that is similar, but not so obvious, as that within Inle's Section 5. Once again, we offer alternative versions for the salute. The salute as it is played today is presented first. Our alternate version is not based on an historical model and should not be taken as a definitive form. Rather, we offer it as a possible way to rectify irregularities in clave.

Because the okónkolo has such a short pattern, one has to compare the iyá and itótele against clave to find the salute's irregularities. Comparing measure 7 with measure 10 reveals that the iyá pattern repeats in a three measure phrase. This means that by the time Section 2 is reached, the ensemble is playing on the wrong half of the clave.

Match this with our alternate Osun transcription. In this case the rhythm played at measure 6 is inserted into the phrase again at measure 10. This lengthens the conversation so that when it ends at Section 2, it is now placed correctly against clave.

The same conversation is done again after Section 2. In our theoretical version once more the conversation falls correctly with the clave. This is not the case in the actual conversation (m.18).[3]

In both versions Section 2-A serves as the ending. Play this section once only and end the rhythm on the final eighth note of the pattern.

Obatalá

Obatalá is relatively easy to play, but is it long and therefore difficult to memorize. Section 1 is interesting for its juxtaposition of implied duple (iyá and itótele) and triple (okónkolo) meter. This, with the slow tempo, gives a stateliness to the rhythm which seems to represent Obatalá's kingly persona. (The same is true when Obatalá comes down to dance. He should never be rushed and is always graceful.)

Conversation 1-A is complete within itself. However, sometimes Conversation 1-B is played as an extension and optional return to Section 1. Notice the iyá flourish in measure 17 that brings back the Section 1 pattern.

The pulse remains constant at Section 6. The half-note equals the old dotted quarter-note.

Obatalá's salute does not last as long as the transcription suggests. While Section 1 and its conversations might be played for a minute or so, none of the other sections should last more than 30 seconds. The salute should end at the conclusion of a Section 7 cycle.

Dadá

There are two particular points of interest in the Dadá salute. First, notice that the iyá pattern in Section 1 (while spread amongst different stroke types) duplicates clave exactly. Second, we have provided two styles of Section 2. The one presented first seems to be the older version, but the second version is most commonly heard today.

Dadá should be ended on the downbeat of Section 1.

Oggué

There are two styles of playing Section 1 of Oggué. Both are popular today. We have no preference for one over the other. The entire Oggué salute including variations lasts no more than 30 seconds. The rhythm is closed on the downbeat of the second measure of the Section 1 pattern.

Agayú

The okónkolo should be careful to lock in the tempo of Sections 1 and 2 as given by the iyá Entrance call. An inexperienced iyá player will tend to rush Agayú if the okónkolo allows it.

The relationship between the tempi of Section 2 (duple) and Section 3 (triple) is found through metric modulation. The value of the eighth note stays the same through both sections.

Section 5 leads back to Section 4 and then goes on to Section 6. After one or two repetitions of Section 6 the piece ends on the first note of the pattern.

Orula

After going into Section 3, iyá brings the group back to Section 2. The salute is closed on the initial downbeat of Section 2.

Oricha Oko

Like the Osun salute, Oricha Oko often begins with a sixteenth note iyá open tone pickup.

Oricha Oko has problems similar to those found in Osun, and again, we offer the alternative theoretical transcription not as a definitive form, but rather as a possible way to rectify irregularities in clave.

Like Osun the length of the Orisha Oko iyá pattern is such that it brings the total cycle into opposition with the clave. The first part of the iya's conversation begins on the back half of measure 5, therefore, when itótele answers, it does so from the back half of measure 6. What is unusual is that in contrast to every occurrence of this itótele pattern in every other salute, the open tone/muffled tone pattern begins on the second half of the measure rather than at the beginning.

Assuming that the itótele response is correct, since the conversation repeats twice, it should begin again in the same place against the clave. However, measure 12 marks the beginning of the second cycle of the conversation and the itótele open tone now falls on the beginning of the measure rather than the back half.

In the Alternate Theoretical Conversation we have changed the Entrance to Conversation and thereby ajusted the first part of the iya's conversation to begin at the start of the clave (mms. 5-7). Now the itótele is sounding its pattern in its usual position. If that were the only change made, that would still throw the second cycle of the conversation out of clave. To rectify this remaining problem, we have expanded the figure in Conversation 1-A of the standard version (the second half of m. 9), taking as a model a similar figure in Conversation 1-B (mms. 21-2), and placed it in Alternate Conversation 1-A (m. 11).

There are similar problems in Conversation 1-B. We believe that the iyá figure found in the standard version (mms. 10, 15-16, 22-23, and 28) should always occur against the second half of the clave. Measures 10 and 28 are correct in this regard. The other appearances do not fit. This is also corrected in the Alternate version of Conversation 1-B. We find that the similarity of the ensemble pattern in Conversation 1-B (mms. 19-21) with Conversation 1-A of Osun (7-8) suggests that the figure should have a common position against the clave. Therefore, in order to shift Conversation 1-B into the proper position, we have moved the first part of the iyá conversation forward half a measure (m. 21).

Oricha Oko ends with a final downbeat slap tacked on to the end of Conversation 1-B.

Ibedyi

The Ibedyi salute has just one section. Some ensembles consider our Variation 1 to be the basic section pattern.

Ibedyi is closed on the Section 1 downbeat.

Changó

There are six variations in Section 1 and we might have chosen to designate any of them as the basic pattern. We chose the one that we did because it has the simplest iyá rhythm and the other patterns might be seen as building in complexity from that matrix. There is no particular order to the way the variations should be played nor is it necessary to play them all.

Section 2 presents another transcription problem. We have chosen to write the rhythm in four, but that is only an approximation of the proper feel. If played in a true four the rhythm is too angular. Therefore, when playing this section soften the sixteenth note divisions just a bit so that the overall sound is rounded.[4]

The tempo increases with each new section. This should not happen during the entrance pattern but at the arrival of the section proper. Of the three tempo changes, the final one at Section 4 is the most difficult because of the time difference. The itótele is very important in establishing the new tempo and should drive the ensemble forward with the slap strokes.

The salute closes on the iyá double stroke at the end of the pattern.

Yegguá

We wrote Yegguá in six but like the Changó salute, it seems to fall somewhere between four and six. Keep this in mind when playing the sixteenth note patterns and consider giving them a slightly lazy feel so that they fall just a bit towards a duple conception.

There is one major discrepancy found in the okónkolo part as played by various ensembles. In measure 13 (bar three of Section 2-A) our transcription shows the okónkolo player returning to the more stable pattern played in Section 1. However, some groups continue with the syncopated okónkolo pattern throughout the entire conversation.

The salute is closed on the Section 1 downbeat.

Oyá

In general, performing the salute to Oyá is self-explanatory. However, there is one area of contention. Ensembles use alternate methods in exiting Section 3, and most of these violate the clave. In addition to the regular transcription, we have included three alternate styles of

Section 3. As with the Inle salute, our basic transcription contains material that has rarely been heard since the 1950s. However, this version has the virtue of remaining true to clave. All of the alternative examples are played today, but none of them uphold clave. In each Alternative Entrance to Section 3, the itótele shifts its backbeat slap to the downbeat. This follows through into the Return to Section 2, so that Section 2 is no longer in the same position against the clave that it was prior to Section 3. Notice the difference in the itótele positions in the new Section 2. Only Alternate Version 3 makes an attempt to rectify this by returning the itótele slap to the backbeat. However, the itótele is now reversed in clave.

Which should you use? While we prefer the older version, performance practice suggests that any of the other three may be more correct.

Oyá is closed by the iyá player striking a double stop (open tone and slap) on the downbeat immediately following Section 5.

Ochún

The Ochún salute has no unusual problems. The salute is closed at the final iyá slap of the Section 1 pattern.

Yemayá

Conversation 1-A is generally repeated enough times that it almost gains the structural importance of a section. After completing Conversation 1-A return to Section 1 and from here go into the Entrance to Section 2. The tempo increases as Section 2 is entered and the tempo gradually increases with each variation that follows until the dotted quarter note reaches a metronome marking of about 168. (This is reflected in the okónkolo touch strokes which are deleted in approximately the place that we have transcribed.)

Variations 2-A and 2-B should not be repeated. Variations 2-C (A-C) should also be played straight through. Then Variation 2-C (B & C) may be repeated in order.

From Variations 2-C go to Variations 2-D (A-C). Again, play the variations straight through and then repeat only B & C.

Nothing unusual occurs in the next few section changes (through Section 6). However, in Section 7, we find that some itótele players continue to play the pattern from the last four measures of the

Entrance to Section 7 (mms. 67-70) rather than switching to what we have transcribed.

After Section 8 the ensemble must return to Section 2 and from there move on (at a reduced speed — dotted quarter equals a metronome marking of about 126) into Section 9. We suggest that Section 10 be played at this reduced tempo, however, some groups return once again to Section 2 and speed the rhythm up as much as possible before ending. The salute ends in Section 10.

Obba

The iyá call for the Obba salute often begins with a sixteenth note open tone pick-up. Other than that, there are no unusual problems. Obba is closed on the downbeat of the Section 4 pattern.

Odudua

The only formal complication with Odudua is the Alternate Iyá Entrance that we have attached at the end of the transcription. The two entrances seem to be equally popular.

In terms of performance, the okónkolo pattern may cause some ensemble difficulties because the pattern tends to be heard as three beats to the measure rather than three tones syncopated over a two beat measure.

Odudua is closed on the downbeat of the Section 1 pattern.

* * * * * * * * *

This completes the Oru del Igbodu.

Footnotes

1. Because of this, we warn against overt counting. Rather, maintain a sense of both clave and the larger metric pulses, then carefully listen to and shape the spaces that occur between the instruments.
2. In fact, because some drummers deny the existence of an implicit clave, they would consider this a moot point. As always, we choose to present musical structure in its most regulated form.
3. Whenever there has been an expansion or contraction within the iyá part, the itótele has been adjusted accordingly. This applies to the Oricha Oko transcription as well.
4. Julio Collazo plays the itótele part of the first two sections on "Conga, Batá y Chequere" from Mongo Santamaria's album "Up From the Roots," Atlantic SD1-621. Careful listening to this will help you find the proper feel.

ELEGGUA

♩. = 63
ENTRANCE
SECTION 1
VARIATION 1-A
CONVERSATION 1-A
VARIATION 1-B

13
13
13
ENTRANCE TO SECTION 2
17
17
17
SECTION 2
ENTRANCE TO SECTION 3
21
21
21
SECTION 3
25
25
25
VARIATION 3-A
ENTRANCE TO SECTION 4

29
29
29
SECTION 4
ENTRANCE TO SECTION 5
33
33
33
SECTION 5
37
37
37

OGÚN

𝅗𝅥 = 112
1
ENTRANCE
SECTION 1
5
VARIATION 1-A
VARIATION 1-B
9
TRANSITION TO ENTRANCE
OPTIONAL ENTRANCE CALL

13
13
13
ENTRANCE TO SECTION 2
SECTION 2
17
17
17
CALL FOR CONVERSATION
CONVERSATION 2-A
21
21
21
RETURN TO SECTION 1
SECTION 1
25
25
25
ENTRANCE TO SECTION 1-B
SECTION 1/B

29
29
29
VARIATION 1/B-1
VARIATION 1/B-2

OCHOSI

13
13
13
SECTION 2
RETURN TO SECTION 1
17
17
17
ENTRANCE TO SECTION 3
21
21
21
25
25
25
SECTION 3
ENTRANCE TO SECTION 4

29
29
29
SECTION 4
33
33
33
37
37
37
ENTRANCE TO SECTION 5
41
41
41
SECTION 5
ENTRANCE TO SECTION 6

45
45
45
SECTION 6
ENTRANCE TO SECTION 7
49
49
49
SECTION 7
CONVERSATION 7-A
53
53
53
ENTRANCE TO SECTION 8
57
57
57
SECTION 8

OBALOKE

♩. = 120
6/8
1
5
9
ENTRANCE
SECTION 1
CONVERSATION 1-A
CONVERSATION 1-B
ENTRANCE TO SECTION 2
SECTION 2

13
13
13
CONVERSATION 2-A
17
17
17
RETURN TO SECTION 1

INLE

𝅗𝅥 = 92
ENTRANCE
SECTION 1
ENTRANCE TO SECTION 2
SECTION 2
SECTION 3
ENTRANCE TO SECTION 4

13
13
13
SECTION 4
ENTRANCE TO SECTION 5
17
17
17
SECTION 5
21
21
21
ALT. SECTION 5
23
23
23

25
25
25
27
27
27

BABALÚ AYÉ (1)

BABALÚ AYÉ (2)

13
13
13
CONVERSATION 1-A
17
17
17
21
21
21

OSAIN

13
13
13
CONVERSATION 1-B
17
17
17
ENTRANCE TO SECTION 2
21
21
21
SECTION 2
25
25
25
ENTRANCE TO SECTION 3

29
29
29 SECTION 3
VARIATION 3-A
33
33
33 VARIATION 3-B
ENTRANCE TO SECTION 4
37
37
37 SECTION 4
VARIATION 4-A
41
41
41 CONVERSATION 4-A

OSUN

13
13
13
SECTION 2
ENTRANCE TO 2-A
17
17
17
CONVERSATION 2-A
21
21
21

OSUN (ALTERNATE VERSION)

13
13
13
SECTION 2
17
17
17
ENTRANCE TO 2-A
CONVERSATION 2-A
21
21
21
25
25
25

OBATALÁ

13
13
13
CONVERSATION 1-B
17
17
17
21
21
21
ENTRANCE TO SECTION 2
25
25
25
SECTION 2

29
29
29
ENTRANCE TO SECTION 3
33
33
33
SECTION 3
37
37
37
SECTION 4
41
41
41
ENTRANCE TO SECTION 5
SECTION 5

45
45
45
ENTRANCE TO SECTION 6
49
49
49
SECTION 6
53
53
53
ENTRANCE TO SECTION 7
57
57
57
SECTION 7

61
61
61
65
65
65
ALTERNATE SECTION 7
69
69
69
73
73
73

DADÁ

13
13
13
ENTRANCE TO SECTION 2
SECTION 2
17
17
17
RETURN TO SECTION 1
21
21
21
ENTRANCE TO SECTION 2
25
25
25
SECTION 2
RETURN TO SECTION 1

29
29
29

OGGUÉ

♩. = 116
ENTRANCE
SECTION 1
VARIATION 1-A
VARIATION 1-B
VARIATION 1-C

13
13
13
VARIATION 1-D
17
17
17
21
21
21
ALTERNATE ENTRANCE
ALTERNATE SECTION 1

AGAYÚ

𝅗𝅥 = 108
1
1
1
1
ENTRANCE
SECTION 1
5
5
5
CONVERSATION 1-A
9
9
9
CONVERSATION 1-B

13
13
13
ENTRANCE TO SECTION 2
SECTION 2
17
17
17
VARIATION 2-A
VARIATION 2-B
21
21
21
ENTRANCE TO SECTION 3
= 76
25
25
25
SECTION 3

29
29
29
ENTRANCE TO SECTION 4
33
33
33
SECTION 4
ENTRANCE TO SECTION 5
37
37
37
SECTION 5
41
41
41
RETURN TO SECTION 4

45
45
45
ENTRANCE TO SECTION 6
SECTION 6
49
49
49
53
53
53
57
57
57

61
61
61

ORULA

17
17
17
ENTRANCE TO SECTION 2
SECTION 2
21
21
21
VARIATION 2-A
ENTRANCE TO SECTION 3
25
25
25
SECTION 3
29
29
29
RETURN TO SECTION 2

ORICHA OKO

♩. = 80
ENTRANCE
SECTION 1
ENTRANCE TO CONVERSATION
CONVERSATION 1-A

13
13
13
17
17
17
CONVERSATION 1-B
21
21
21
25
25
25

ORICHA OKO (ALTERNATE VERSION)

13
13
13
17
17
17
SECTION 1
21
21
21
CONVERSATION 1-B
25
25
25

29
29
29

IBÉDYI

VARIATION 1-B

CHANGÓ

♩. = 76
ENTRANCE
SECTION 1
VARIATION 1-A
VARIATION 1-B
VARIATION 1-C
VARIATION 1-D

13
13
13
VARIATION 1-E
VARIATION 1-F
17
17
17
ENTRANCE TO SECTION 2
𝅗𝅥 = 88
21
21
21
SECTION 2
VARIATION 2-A
25
25
25
VARIATION 2-B
ENTRANCE TO SECTION 3

♩. = 𝅗𝅥
♩. = 92
29
29
29
SECTION 3
33
33
33
VARIATION 3-A
37
37
37
VARIATION 3-B
41
41
41
ENTRANCE TO SECTION 4

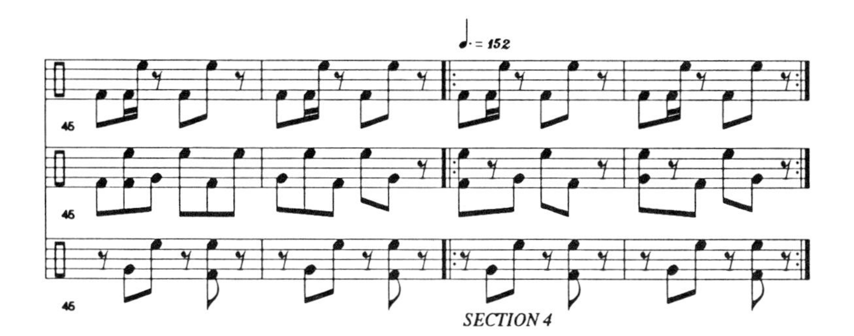
♩. = 152
45
45
45
SECTION 4

YEGGUÁ

♩. = 112
ENTRANCE
SECTION 1
SECTION 2
VARIATION 2-A
VARIATION 2-B
CONVERSATION 2-A

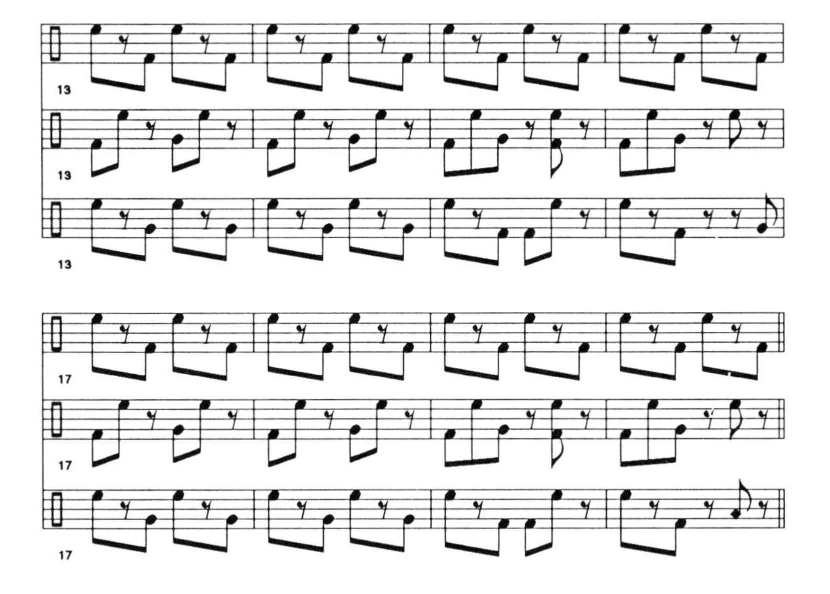
13
13
13
17
17
17

OYA

𝅗𝅥 = 108
1
1
1
1
ENTRANCE
SECTION 1
5
5
5
VARIATION 1-A
ENTRANCE TO CONVERSATION
9
9
9
CONVERSATION 1-A
RETURN TO SECTION 1

13
13
13
ENTRANCE TO SECTION 2
17
17
17
SECTION 2
ENTRANCE TO SECTION 3
21
21
21
SECTION 3
RETURN TO SECTION 2
25
25
25
ENTRANCE TO SECTION 4
SECTION 4

29
29
29
ENTRANCE TO SECTION 5
33
33
33
37
37
37
SECTION 5
41
41
41

45
45
45
ENTRANCE TO SECTION 3
SECTION 3
49
49
49
RETURN TO SECTION 2
SECTION 2
53
53
53
ENTRANCE TO SECTION 3
SECTION 3
57
57
57
RETURN TO SECTION 2
SECTION 2

61
61
61
ENTRANCE TO SECTION 3
SECTION 3
65
65
65
RETURN TO SECTION 2
69
69
69
SECTION 2

OCHÚN

𝅗𝅥 = 100
ENTRANCE
SECTION 1
VARIATION 1-A
VARIATION 1-B
CONVERSATION 1-A

13
13
13

YEMAYÁ

♩. = 54
ENTRANCE
SECTION 1
CONVERSATION 1-A
RETURN TO SECTION 1
ENTRANCE TO SECTION 2

13
13
13
ENTRANCE EXTENSION
17
17
17
SECTION 2
VARIATION 2-A
21
21
21
25
25
25
VARIATION 2-B

29
29
29
33
33
33
VARIATION 2-C (A)
VARIATION 2-C (B)
37
37
37
VARIATION 2-C (C)
VARIATION 2-D (A)
41
41
41
VARIATION 2-D (B)
VARIATION 2-D (C)

45
45
45
ENTRANCE TO SECTION 3
SECTION 3
49
49
49
ENTRANCE TO SECTION 4
SECTION 4
53
53
53
ENTRANCE TO SECTION 5
SECTION 5
57
57
57
CONVERSATION 5-A

61
61
61
ENTRANCE TO SECTION 6
SECTION 6
65
65
65
ENTRANCE TO SECTION 7
69
69
69
SECTION 7
73
73
73
ENTRANCE TO SECTION 8

77
77
77
SECTION 8
81
81
81
RETURN TO SECTION 2
85
85
85
ENTRANCE TO SECTION 9
89
89
89
SECTION 9

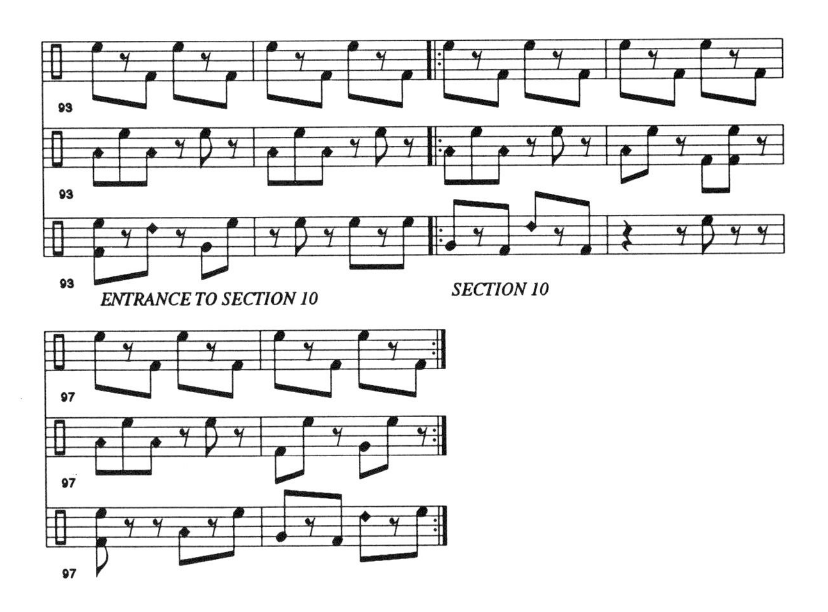
93
93
93
ENTRANCE TO SECTION 10
SECTION 10
97
97
97

OBBA

= 80
ENTRANCE
SECTION 1
ENTRANCE TO SECTION 2
SECTION 2
VARIATION 1-A

13
13
13
ENTRANCE TO SECTION 3
17
17
17
SECTION 3
21
21
21
25
25
25
ENTRANCE TO SECTION 4

29
29
29
33
33
33
SECTION 4
37
37
37
VARIATION 4-A
VARIATION 4-B

ODUDUA

13
13
13
17
17
17
21
21
21
25
25
25
RETURN TO SECTION 1
ALTERNATE ENTRANCE

Appendix I

Glossary of Lucumí and Spanish Terms

Achere — (Lu.) A small rattle which is sometimes used to play the standard bell pattern in batá ensembles.

Agbé — (Lu.) A calabash gourd idiophone strung on the outside with beads. Sometimes called *shekere.*

Agogo — (Lu.) Metal bell used to play the standard bell pattern in bembé ensembles.

Aña — (Lu.) A sacred force believed to reside in the batá drums, considered an oricha by some Santeros.

Batalero — (Lu./Sp.) A batá drummer.

Bembé — (Lu.) A religious party held to honor an oricha.

Cabildo — (Sp.) Mutual aid societies established by slaves in Cuba.

Caminos — (Sp.) Roads. Diferent avatars of an oricha. Each "standard pattern" or toque signifies a different camino.

Chachá — (Lu.) The smaller head of the batá drum.

Chaguoro — (Lu.) Bells wrapped around the shell of the iyá ilú.

Cierre — (Sp.) Closing. The ritual that closes a bembé.

Conversacíon — (Sp.) A conversation that takes place between the iyá and itótele. Conversations used to render lexical meaning but most of this knowledge has been lost.

Enú — (Lu.) The larger head of the batá drum.

Fardela — (Sp.) Also called the idá, it is a ring of clay molded to the iyá ilú. It is used to dampen the drum's overtones.

Güiro — (Sp.) Musical gourd. An idiophone, it is also known as agbé or shekere. It is covered with strung beads and played by shaking and striking the bottom.

Idá — (Lu.) See Fardela.

Itótele — (Lu.) The middle drum of the batá set.

Iyá — (Lu.) Mother.

Iyá Ilú — (Lu.) Mother drum. The lead drum in the batá ensemble.

Llame — (Sp.) The call used in batá drumming to begin a rhythm or initiate a conversation.

Lucumí — Name used to identify Yoruba slaves and their language in Cuba. Practitioners today sometimes call their religion Lucumí.

Ocha — (Lu.) A saint/oricha. The religion of Santería (Regla de Ocha).

Okónkolo — (Lu.) The smallest drum of the batá set. Also called omelé.

Olori — (Lu.) The strap used by the batalero to secure the drum during performance.

Olú Batá — (Lu.) A batalero initiated into Aña.

Omelé — (Lu.) Another name for okónkolo.

Omo — (Lu.) Child.

Ori — (Lu.) The physical head and inner person. The essence of personality.

Oricha — (Lu.) Sacred head. The nature divinities of traditional Yoruba religion and Santería.

Oru — (Lu.) A liturgical sequence of songs or batá rhythms. (Sometimes mistakenly called oro.)

Oru del Igbodu — (Lu.) "Oru in front of the throne" played on the batá drums without song. Also called oru seco.

Orun — (Lu.) The heaven world of Yoruba religion.

Santería — (Sp.) The Lucumí religion of Cuba.

Santero, Santera — (Sp.) Male and female initiates or priests of Santería.

Santo — (Sp.) Saint. The oricha.

Tambor — (Sp.) Drummer.

Tamabor — (Sp.) Drum.

— A liturgical fiesta for the orichas using the batá drums.

Toque — (Sp.) A batá rhythm.

— Another name for a liturgical fiesta using batá.

Yesa — (Lu.) Single headed drum type found in Cuba.

— Name of generic rhythms played in "drum and güiro" ensembles. In batá ensembles this rhythm is called rumba yesa.

Appendix II

Discography

Aché. Merceditas Valdez. Egrem LV 230.
Afro Tambores Batá. Orfeon LP-LAB-08.
Antologia de la Musica Afrocubana. Vol. II: Oru De Igbodu. (1981) EGREM. Ciudad de la Habana, Cuba. Catalogue #: LD-3995. (While the rhythms are very clear on this album they are in the Matanzas batá style rather than the Havana /New York style.)
Bembé. (1986) Milton Cardona and the Eya Aranla Ensemble. American Clave, 213 E. 11th St., New York, NY. Catalogue #: American Clave 1004.
Conjunto Folklorico Nacional. Areito. LDA 3156.
Cuba. Philips 844948BY.
Cuba: Musique Afro-Cubaine. Dissques Alvarés LD 453.
Cuban and Puerto Rican Music from the African and Hispanic Traditions. From the "Voices of the Americas Series." The World Music Institute, 109 West 27th St., New York, NY. Catalogue #: T-111. Also available through: Music of the World, P.O. Box 258, Brooklyn, NY 11209.
Cult Music of Cuba. Folkways Records FE 4410.
Ecos Afro-Cubanos. Orfeon LP-12-138.
Merceditas Valdes. Panart LD 3096.
Misa Santería. Riviera 521-107.
Mongo in Havana. Fantasy 3311.
Ritmo de Santo. Maype US-130.
Ritmo y Lamento. CHB Records 417.
Rhythmes de Cuba. Les Chante du Monde LD-5-4218.
Santería (Toques y Cantos). Grupo folklorico de Justi Barreto. Gema Records Corp. LPG 1193.
Santero #1. Panart Records LP-2060.
Santero #2. Panart Records LP-2097.
Toques y Cantos de Santos. Cubilandia 511.
Up From the Roots: Mongo Santamaria. 1972. Atlantic 501-621
Viejos Cantos Afro-Cubanos. Areito LD 3325.

Annotated Bibliography

There is a relative lack of research in English on the present state of New World batá drumming. However, should you wish to explore this music or the religious beliefs further, the following guide may help direct your initial research.

Serious study of the music of Santería began with the Cuban scholar, Fernando Ortiz. His work is seminal not only for initiating research on this previously undocumented tradition, but also for inadvertently influencing the development of religious drumming in New York City. His five volume set on the musical instruments of Afro-Cuba (1952-5) is outstanding in terms of both classification and completeness, while his transcriptions of rhythms and song texts (1965, 1974, 1981) are commonly found in the libraries of New York musicians and Santeros. The works of Carpentier (1940) and Leon (1964), while much less extensive, document the musics of various ethnic groups of African descent in Cuba. Cabrera's works (1980a, 1980b, 1983) are primary sources for the understanding of religious conception. Her Lucumí/Spanish dictionary (1970) includes valuable information for song texts. Although the works by two practicing Santeros (Garcia Cortez and Ramos) are less scholarly than the above citations, they are nevertheless useful for their insider perspectives. Garcia Cortez (1971) discusses numerous aspects of the religion and provides some song texts. Ramos (n.d.) concentrates on song texts, however, he provides no melodies or translations. Both books are popular amongst musicians and Santeros.

There are also a number of important studies published in English. The early works of Herskovits (1937) and later research of Bascom (1972) and Bastide (1971) provide excellent introductions to African religious retention in the New World. Courlander (1942) and Howard (1967) discuss the musical instruments of Cuba. Friedman (1982) has done the only New York-based music research prior to our work and while providing a general introduction to music ritual, the study appears to have been written under considerable restrictions imposed by his informants (Friedman 1982:xi-xii). Thompson's work (1983) provides considerable insight into the Afro-American experience, relating contemporary aesthetic goals with West African cultural and religious conceptions. Of related interest, Stuckey (1987) documents African cultural retention in the United States. Many of his examples deal with music.

Babar, Karin
1981 "How man makes god in West Africa: Yoruba attitudes toward the orisa," *Africa* 51:3 724-745.
Barnes, Sandra T.
1980 *Ogun: an old God for a new age.* Philadelphia Institute for the Study of Human Issues.
Bascom, William
1972 *Shango in the New World.* African and Afro-American Research Institute. Austin: University of Texas.
Cabrera, Lydia
1970 *Anago: Vocabulario Lucuna (El Yoruba se hable in Cuba).* Miami: Editiones, C.R.
1980a *Koeko Iyawo: Aprende Novicia.* Miami: Ultra Graphics Corporation.
1980b *Yemaya y Ochun.* NY: C.R., Eastchester, NY: Distribution esclusiva E. Torres.
1983 *El Monte: Igbo Finda Ewe Orisha.* Miami: Coleccion del Chichereku. (1954 Havana: Editiones C.R.).
Castellanos, Isabel M.
1977 *Use of Language in Afro-Cuban Religion.* Ph.D. dissertation, Georgetown University.
Courlander, Harold
1942 "Musical Instruments of Cuba," *Musical Quarterly* 28:2: 227-240.
Eades, J.S.
1980 *The Yoruba Today.* Cambridge: Cambridge University Press.
Edwards, Gary and John Mason
1985 *Black Gods—Orisha Studies in the New World.* U.S.A.: Yoruba Theological Seminary.
Fadipe, N.A.
1970 *The Sociology of the Yoruba.* Ibadan: University of Ibadan Press.
Friedman, Robert
1982 Making an Abstract World Concrete: Knowledge, Competence and Structural Dimensions of Performance Among Batá Drummers in Santería. Ph.D. dissertation, Indiana University.
Garcia Cortez, Julio
1971 *El Santo (La Ocha): Secretos de la Religion Lucumí.* Miami: Editiones Universal.

Gonzalez-Wippler, Migene
1973 *Santería: African Magic in Latin America.* New York: The Julian Press, Inc. (1981 Original Publications.)
Herskovits, Melville
1937 "African gods and Catholic saints in new world Negro belief," *American Anthropologist* 139.
Howard, Joseph H.
1967 *Drums in the Americas.* New York: Oak Publications.
Idowu, E. Bolaji
1962 *Olodumare: God in Yoruba Belief.* Nigeria: Longman Nigeria Unlimited.
Klein, Herbert S.
1967 *Slavery in the Americas: A Comparative Study of Virginia and Cuba.* Chicago: University of Chicago Press.
Knight, Franklin W.
1970 *Slave Society in Cuba During the Nineteenth Century.* Milwaukee and London: University of Wisconsin Press.
Lawson, E. Thomas
1984 *Religions of Africa.* New York: Harper & Row.
Leon, Argeliers
1964 *Musica Folklorica Cubana.* Havana: Biblioteca Nacional Jose Marti.
Omibiyi, Mosunmula
1978 The Training of Yoruba Traditional Musicians. In, *Yoruba Oral Tradition: Poetry in Music, Dance ad Drama.* Edited by Wande Abimbola. Ibadan, Nigeria: Department of African Language and Literature, University of Ife.
Ortiz, Fernando
1952 & 1954 *Los Instrumentos de la musica Afrocubana.* Volumes III & IV. Havana: Ministerio de Educacion.
1965 *La Africania de la Musica Folklorica de Cuba.*
1974 *La Musica Afro-Cubana.* Madrid: Editiones Jucar.
1981 *Los bailes y el teatro de los negros en el folklore de Cuba.* [1951]. Havana: Editorial Letral Cubanas. 603p.
Parrinder, G.
1961 *West African Religion.* London: The Epworth Press.
Ramos, Willie
N.D. *Ase Omo Osayin Ewe Aye.* (No copyright information.)

Stuckey, Sterling
1987 *Slave Culture: Nationalist theory and the Foundations of Black America.* New York: Oxford University Press.
Thompson, Robert Farris
1984 *Flash of the Spirit.* U.S.A.: Random House.

Index

Aché, definition, 7
Agayú
  aspects, 8
  musical analysis, 23,43
Agbé, 21
Aguabella, Francisco, 10
Babalú Ayé, 22-23
  aspects, 7
  musical analysis, 40

Batá, 1-3, 10-13
  history, 13
  taboos, 13
  construction, 15-16
  symbolism, 18
  speech, 21-22
  instrumental roles, 23-26
  technique, 35-40
Bembé, definition, 21-22

Cabildo, 6
Chachá, 15, 17
  tuning, 27, 36
Changó, 8, 9, 15-16, 23
  musical analysis, 45
Cierre, 22
Clave, 23-24, 26, 35, 36, 38, 39-46
Collazo, Julio, 10-11
construction, 15-17
conversation, 24-26, 33, 36-37, 41- 46

Dadá, 8, 23
  musical analysis, 43

Eléggua, 7, 22-23
  musical analysis, 37

Enú, 15, 32, 36
  tuning, 17-18

Fardela, 18

Güiro, 21-22

Ibedyi, 8, 23
  musical analysis, 44
Idá, 18
Ifa (see Orula)
Inle, 7, 23, 36
  musical analysis, 40
Itótele, 11, 15, 24-25,32, 36-42, 44-46
  performance role, 26
Iyá, 11, 15-16, 24, 25-29, 40-47
  tuning, 17-18
  performance role, 25-27
  striking, 32

Llame, 24

Obaloke, 7, 23
  musical analysis, 42
Obatálá, 7, 8, 23
  musical analysis, 42
Obba, 9, 23
  musical analysis, 47
Ochosi, 7, 23, 38
  musical analysis, 39
Ochún, 8, 9, 16, 23
  musical analysis, 46
Odudua, 9, 23
  musical analysis, 47
Oggué, 8, 23
  musical analysis, 43
Ogún, 7, 16, 23
  musical analysis, 38

Okónkolo, 11, 15, 17-18, 24-25, 27, 36, 38, 40-47
  performance role, 26
  striking, 32
Olori, 27
Olorun, 5-6
Omelé, 15
Oricha, 1-2, 5, 13, 18, 38, 40, 43-44
  definition and list, 6-8
  honoring through performance, 21-23
Oricha Oko, 8, 23
  musical analysis, 43-44
Oríki, 22, 24
Ortiz, Fernando, 11-12, 22, 39
Oru del Igbodu, 2, 21-23, 40, 47
Orula, 8, 22-23
  musical analysis, 43
Osain, 7, 22-23,
  musical analysis, 41
Osun, 8, 23, 43-44
  musical analysis, 43-44
Oyá, 8-9, 22-23
  musical analysis, 45-46

Pozo, Chano, 10

Rios, Orlando Puntilla, 12
Roads, 7, 22, 24

Santamaria, Mongo, 10
symbolism, 18

Tambor, 21-22
Toque, 21
Transcription key, 36
tuning, 16-18

Valdez, Patato, 10

Yegguá, 8, 22-23
  musical analysis, 45
Yemayá, 8, 9, 22-23
  musical analysis, 26

Batá drum sets are available from White Cliffs!

Photograph by Martin Cohen, Latin Percussion™

✔As a service to our readers White Cliffs Media is proud to offer for sale a complete set of Batá drums. These drums, made of Siam oak, were designed with the help of author John Amira and manufactured with state-of-the-art machinery by Latin Percussion™.

The shapes of the shells are gracefully tapered, and the shell thickness increases at the smallest point of the drum in order to increase the strength and improve sound quality. Each Batá drum is supplied with a neck strap, tuning wrench, and lug lube. Replacement heads and rims are available. Each drum is guaranteed for six months, excluding drum heads and abnormal use. 5% discount is available when ordering all three drums as a set.

# M92490	Iyá (Large drum)	$512.95
# M92491	Itótele (Medium drum)	$479.95
# M92492	Okonkolo (Small drum)	$454.95

We accept advance payment by check, Visa, Mastercard or American Express. Prices are subject to change and will be verified before shipment. Any returns must be prompt, undamaged and are subject to a 15% restocking fee. Drums are shipped UPS with shipping at cost charged COD. Send orders with check or credit card info to White Cliffs Media, P.O. Box 561, Crown Point, IN 46307. For ORDERS ONLY, call 1-800-359-3210.